WHEN DISASTER STRIKES

EXTREME HURRICANES AND TORNADOES

Thanks to the creative team:

Senior Editor: Alice Peebles
Fact checking: Tom Jackson
Illustration: Jeremy Pyke
Picture Research: Nic Dean
Design: www.collaborate.agency

First published in Great Britain in 2017
by Hungry Tomato Ltd
PO Box 181
Edenbridge
Kent, TN8 9DP

A CIP catalogue record for this book is
available from the British Library.

ISBN 978-1-912108-70-1

Printed and bound in China

Discover more at
www.hungrytomato.com

WHEN DISASTER STRIKES

EXTREME HURRICANES AND TORNADOES

by John Farndon

HUNGRY TOMATO.

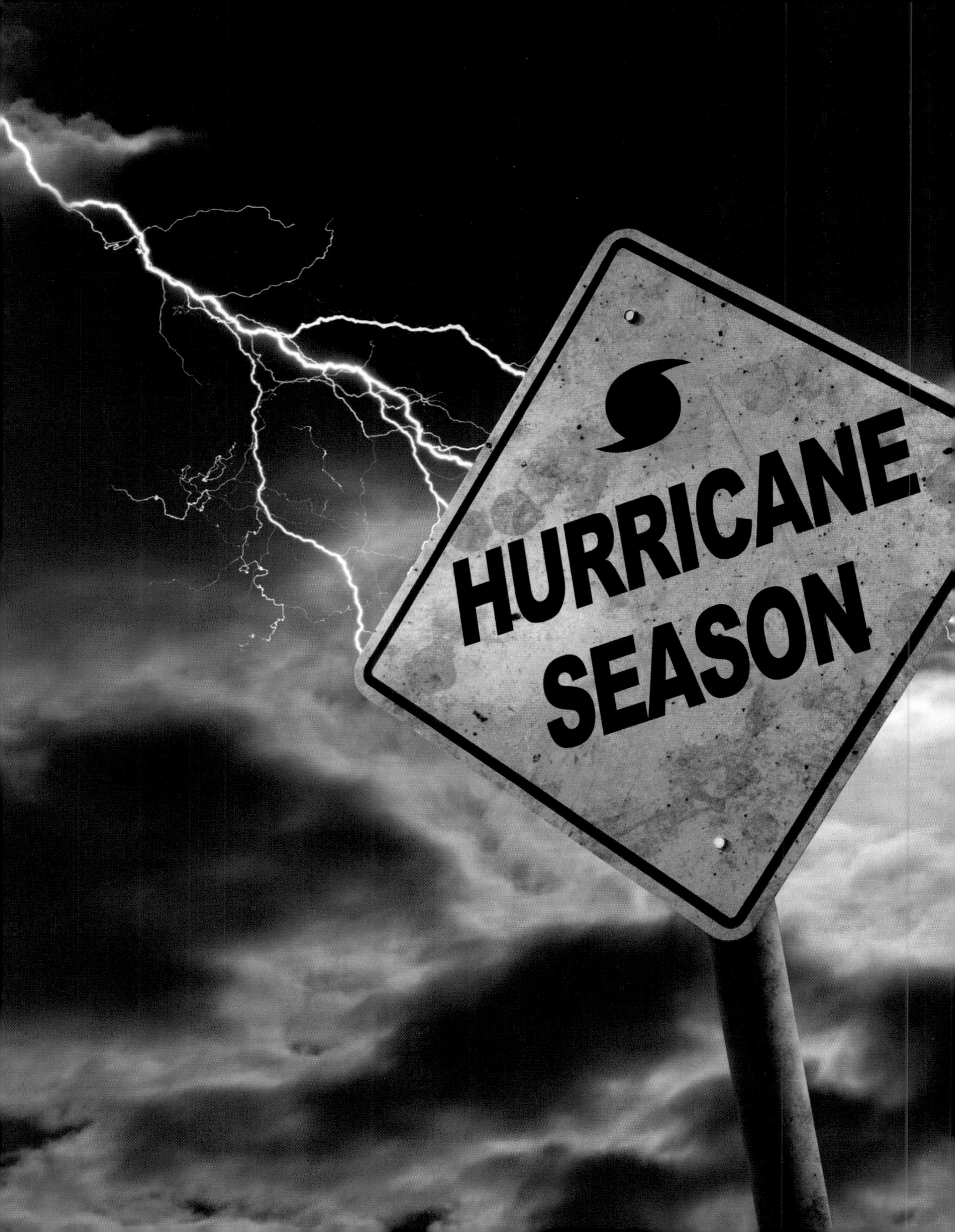
HURRICANE
SEASON

CONTENTS

HURRICANES

A hurricane is a storm so vast you can only see it all from space. From high above, it looks like a huge whirling cream cake. The white is rings of huge, powerful thunderclouds that bring torrential rain. The whirls are created by powerful winds that blow in a spiral round the storm's centre or 'eye'.

'Hurricane' is the name given to a spiralling tropical storm in the Atlantic Ocean. Similar storms may also be called typhoons in the Pacific. Scientists call them both 'tropical cyclones'.

TORNADOES

Tornadoes, also known as twisters and whirlwinds, are spinning, roaring columns of air just a few hundred metres across. They come down from giant thunderclouds and rip across the landscape, destroying buildings, uprooting trees and hurling cars in the air. Winds spiral around the outside at ferocious speeds — while pressure in the centre is so low it can suck objects up like a giant vacuum cleaner.

HOW DOES A HURRICANE HAPPEN?

Hurricanes are stirred into life in late summer by tropical sun beating down on the ocean and steaming off water to build giant thunderclouds. High above, strong winds blow from the east. The winds skim the cloud tops and swirl them together in one big spiral storm. The storm wheels westwards, gaining power as it gathers in more clouds.

UNBELIEVABLE!
According to NASA, a hurricane can expend as much energy during its life cycle as 10,000 nuclear bombs!

CROSS-SECTION OF A HURRICANE

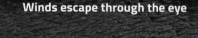

Rotating cloud mass

In the very centre of the eye, air sinks again, creating a brief moment of clear skies and calm weather

EYE

Winds escape through the eye

Winds roar round anticlockwise at sea level

ANATOMY OF A HURRICANE

In a hurricane, rain lashes down from rings of thunderstorms known as rainbands, while howling winds at sea level drive the storm anticlockwise. Right in the centre there is a clear tunnel up through the clouds, called the 'eye', where winds spiral up the cloud walls and out.

WHIRL OF POWER

A big hurricane releases as much energy in a day as all the world's power stations in a year. The power comes from all the thunderclouds clustered together in a spiral of cloud rings hundreds of miles across.

Rainband

STORM FROM AFRICA

In the Atlantic, hurricanes typically begin off Africa, near the Cape Verde islands. As they develop, they move west over the ocean at about 24 km/h (15 mph). In under two weeks, they hit the Caribbean and swing northwards. By this time they are at the height of their power.

Hurricanes

Equator

HURRICANE FORCE

Hurricanes create superstrong winds. To be classed as a hurricane, a storm must have winds of at least 118 km/h (74 mph), known as 'hurricane force' winds. But in a powerful hurricane, winds can get much stronger. In Hurricane Camille in 1969, winds reached 305 km/h (190 mph)!

A HURRICANE'S BIRTHPLACE

Hurricanes begin just north or south of the Equator on the eastern edge of all three major tropical oceans: the Atlantic, Indian and Pacific. They sweep westwards as they develop, then swing away from the Equator before finally petering out.

HITTING LAND

It's once they hit land that hurricanes really do their damage. Long before the storm arrives, huge waves stirred up by the wind start to smash against the coast. Then watchers on the shore see ominous dark clouds heading their way, and feel the wind picking up. They're in for a rough time!

HURRICANE IN HAITI

When Hurricane Matthew hit Haiti (main picture and inset) in 2007, the winds were strong enough to bend even the strongest trees, and blow roofs off all but the stoutest buildings, while torrential rains brought instant flooding. Hurricane winds are often strong enough to blow away a big car.

TRICKED!

After six hours of battering, the onslaught may often seem to die down. The rain stops. The wind drops. The sun may come out. But this is a brief respite as the eye of the storm passes over. Within an hour, the eye has moved on and the rain and wind come storming back.

STORM SURGE

Low air pressure in the hurricane's eye lifts the ocean surface up in a dome. Winds pile up water even higher. This is called a 'storm surge'. As the hurricane moves landwards, it drives the surge with it, creating a massive high tide that can swamp coastal areas and sweep far inland.

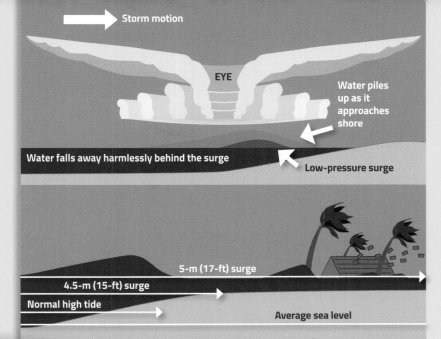

Storm motion

EYE

Water piles up as it approaches shore

Water falls away harmlessly behind the surge

Low-pressure surge

5-m (17-ft) surge

4.5-m (15-ft) surge

Normal high tide

Average sea level

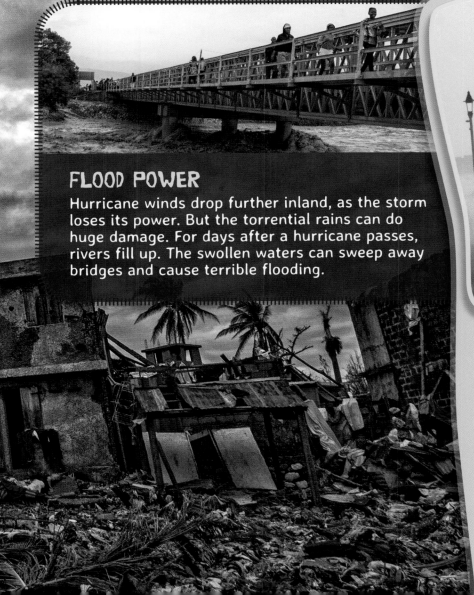

FLOOD POWER

Hurricane winds drop further inland, as the storm loses its power. But the torrential rains can do huge damage. For days after a hurricane passes, rivers fill up. The swollen waters can sweep away bridges and cause terrible flooding.

WAVE POWER

Coasts exposed to hurricanes take a real battering from giant waves. When Hurricane Ivan hit the Atlantic coast of the USA on 15 September 2004, it threw up waves over 27 m (90 ft) high. Just imagine a wall of water as high as a 10-storey building coming at you!

EXTREME HURRICANE DAMAGE

Some hurricanes cause little more than inconvenience. But the most powerful can be hugely destructive, especially if they hit areas where a lot of people live. The ferocious winds can destroy buildings and power lines, while the floods from the heavy rain can wash away bridges, cut off roads and railways, and trap people.

UNBELIEVABLE!
A slower-moving, weaker hurricane can often do more damage than a faster-moving, more powerful one, because it stays long enough to drop heavy rain and cause flooding.

SANDY MONSTER
Hurricane Sandy of October 2012 (main picture) was the biggest hurricane ever, measuring 1,800 km (1,100 miles) across. It caused at least $75 billion damage when it hit land everywhere from Jamaica to New York — second only to Hurricane Katrina.

GALVESTON CALAMITY
On 8 September 1900, the city of Galveston in Texas (right), then the 'New York of the South', was utterly destroyed when a hurricane ripped through it. The 225-km/h (140-mph) winds flattened many buildings, while a 4.5-m (15-ft) storm surge washed them away. More than 6,000 people died and 3,600 buildings were totally destroyed.

BANGLADESH

FLOOD TERROR

More than half of Bangladesh lies less than 6 m (20 ft) above sea level. Worse still, the shape of the Bay of Bengal means storm surges are funnelled towards the country's low-lying coast. So cyclones have repeatedly brought floods to Bangladesh, with devastating effects.

SHIP TO SHORE

There were few better shows of the power of Hurricane Sandy than the appearance of a 52-m (170-ft) tanker on Front St on New York's Staten Island. The ship had been anchored a mile out in the bay, but was hurled onshore by the storm.

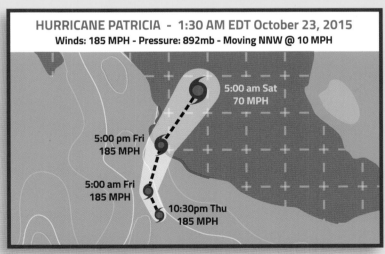

JOHN B. CADDELL

HURRICANE PATRICIA - 1:30 AM EDT October 23, 2015
Winds: 185 MPH - Pressure: 892mb - Moving NNW @ 10 MPH

5:00 am Sat
70 MPH

5:00 pm Fri
185 MPH

5:00 am Fri
185 MPH

10:30pm Thu
185 MPH

POWERHOUSE PATRICIA

October 2015's Hurricane Patricia was the second most intense hurricane ever — with the second lowest pressures ever recorded, at its centre. It also hit land in Mexico with winds more ferocious than any other hurricane. Fortunately, Patricia ran straight into mountains and rural areas, so did much less damage than if it had hit a city.

13

EXTREME HURRICANE STORY

No one who lived in New Orleans, Louisiana, in August 2005 will ever forget Hurricane Katrina. It was one of the deadliest, and certainly the costliest, natural disasters ever to hit the USA. More than 1,800 people lost their lives, and estimates put the cost of the damage at well over $100 billion.

UNBELIEVABLE!
The storm surge from Katrina was a massive 5–9 m (15–30 ft), the highest ever recorded in the USA.

BURST BANKS
Low-lying New Orleans relies on banks called 'levees' to keep water within its waterways. But during Katrina, the storm surge and heavy rain combined to fill the waterways to bursting. Soon water spilled over the levees, then breached them altogether in 50 different places, flooding the city.

DEMOLITION
These pictures show a beach house in New Orleans before and after Katrina hit. Altogether, over a million homes were damaged, 134,000 in New Orleans alone — that's nearly three-quarters of all homes in the city. The main cause of the damage was flooding.

HEAT POWER

When Katrina arrived in the Gulf of Mexico it was a mild hurricane. But the unusually warm waters there intensified it dramatically. The storm doubled in size and went from Category 3 to Category 5 (see p. 17) in just nine hours. Katrina was one of only four Category 5 hurricanes ever to hit the USA.

THE BIG EASY

When Katrina struck, New Orleans was a bustling city where almost half a million people lived. But as the hurricane approached, many people evacuated and 80 per cent of the city was flooded. A year later, barely 200,000 had come back, leaving the city a shadow of itself.

ONE STEP AHEAD OF THE HURRICANE

Every year between June and November, 10 hurricanes sweep across the Atlantic – and one or two strike the coast of the USA. This is the hurricane season and the National Hurricane Centre in Florida is on high alert to track developing hurricanes and give people as much warning as possible.

UNBELIEVABLE!

Hurricane Hunters (see right) sometimes fly right through the hurricane's eye wall, the most intense part of the storm! The planes are lashed by driving rain and hail, battered by winds of 240 km/h (155 mph) or more, and tossed by violent updrafts and downdrafts.

SPACE EYE VIEW

Scientists can follow the path of hurricanes easily from satellites high above. By putting several hours of satellite pictures together, they can see how it is developing. But hurricanes can change path very quickly. This is Hurricane Matthew threatening Florida in October 2016.

THE HURRICANE HUNTERS

Drones, or robot aircraft, can be guided into a hurricane by remote-control. They can be sent to monitor conditions in the most dangerous parts of a hurricane without putting aircrew's lives at risk. Drones can fly for 30 hours at twice the height of a passenger plane.

RAIN CHECK

Doppler radar detects things by bouncing microwaves off them. With a special kind of Doppler radar, hurricane watchers can build up a detailed map of where and how much rain is falling. It can even give an indication of wind speed. This radar station is located in Dodge City, Kansas.

HURRICANE SCALE

The strength of a hurricane is graded in categories from 1 to 5 on the Saffir-Simpson hurricane wind scale.

Category	Wind Speed	Damage	
1	74–95 mph (119–153 km/h)	Light damage: mobile homes shifted; signs blown over; branches broken	
2	96–110 mph (154–177 km/h)	Moderate damage: mobile homes turned over; roofs lifted	
3	111–129 mph (178–208 km/h)	Extensive damage: small buildings wrecked; trees uprooted	
4	130–156 mph (209–251 km/h)	Extreme damage: most trees blown down; widespread structural damage to all buildings	
5	Above 157 mph (252 km/h)	Catastrophic damage: most buildings destroyed; forests, roads and pipelines wrecked	

HOW DOES A TORNADO HAPPEN?

The most dangerous place in the world for tornadoes is Tornado Alley, which stretches across North America's Great Plains. Here, warm air from the Gulf of Mexico collides with cold winds blowing from the Rocky Mountains. This creates huge thunderstorms called supercells, which are like mighty tornado makers.

UNBELIEVABLE!

Typically the winds whipping round a tornado are about 160 km/h (100 mph). But sometimes they can reach as much as 480 km/h (300 mph) and have the power to pick up a log and hurl it through a brick wall!

BANGS AND FLASHES

The approach of a tornado is terrifying. The spinning winds roar like a very loud freight train, while thunderclaps boom and lightning flashes from the cloud above. Fortunately, they only tend to last 10 minutes or so before petering out.

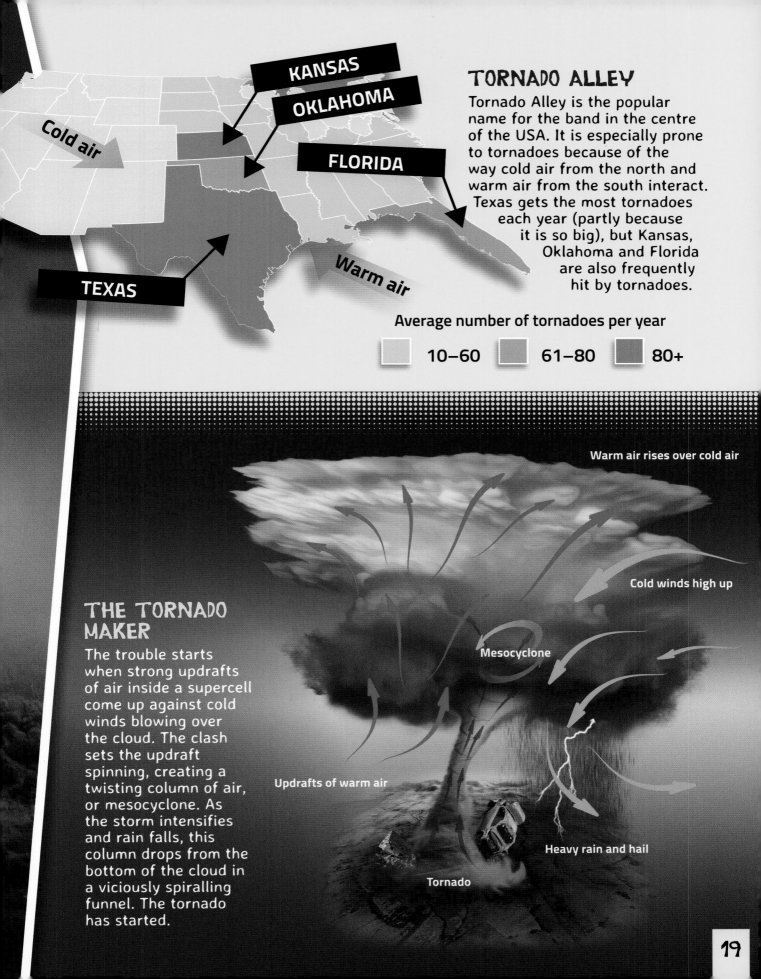

TORNADO ALLEY

Tornado Alley is the popular name for the band in the centre of the USA. It is especially prone to tornadoes because of the way cold air from the north and warm air from the south interact. Texas gets the most tornadoes each year (partly because it is so big), but Kansas, Oklahoma and Florida are also frequently hit by tornadoes.

KANSAS

OKLAHOMA

FLORIDA

TEXAS

Cold air

Warm air

Average number of tornadoes per year

10–60   61–80   80+

THE TORNADO MAKER

The trouble starts when strong updrafts of air inside a supercell come up against cold winds blowing over the cloud. The clash sets the updraft spinning, creating a twisting column of air, or mesocyclone. As the storm intensifies and rain falls, this column drops from the bottom of the cloud in a viciously spiralling funnel. The tornado has started.

Warm air rises over cold air

Cold winds high up

Mesocyclone

Updrafts of warm air

Heavy rain and hail

Tornado

EXTREME TORNADO DAMAGE

Often, tornadoes whirl by doing little damage, apart from shaking a tree or blowing a loose door off its hinges. But sometimes they cause catastrophic damage, blasting buildings flat, hurling cars through the air, and killing and injuring people and animals. The severity of a tornado is measured from 0 to 5 on the Enhanced Fujita scale.

UNBELIEVABLE!

The deadliest tornado in US history occurred on 18 March 1925. It killed 695 people and travelled more than 480 km (300 miles) through Missouri, Illinois and Indiana. The storm was rated an F5 on the Fujita scale.

HOUSE DOWN

This house in Joplin, Missouri, blown apart in May 2011 by an EF5 tornado, reveals the destructive power of tornadoes. Curiously, books are left neatly stacked on the shelves, showing just how localized the effects can be.

EXTREME STORY: RAINING FROGS

Amazingly, rainstorms can often bring showers of frogs as well as water! The theory is that they are picked up by tornadoes skimming over ponds. Tornadoes that form over water, known as waterspouts, can even pick up fish!

TORNADO SCALE

The damage done by a tornado is rated from 0 to 5 on the Enhanced Fujita scale.

Scale	Wind Speed	Damage
EF0	65–85 mph (105–137 km/h)	Minor damage: roof tiles disturbed; branches of trees broken
EF1	86–110 mph (138–177 km/h)	Moderate damage: roof tiles torn off; mobile homes overturned; cars blown off roads
EF2	111–135 mph (178–217 km/h)	Considerable damage: roofs blown off; mobile homes destroyed; railway trucks overturned; large trees uprooted
EF3	136–165 mph (218–266 km/h)	Severe damage: houses blown down; cars hurled through the air; heavy objects flung like missiles
EF4	166–200 mph (267–322 km/h)	Extreme damage: houses, even with strong foundations, destroyed; cars turned into flying missiles; trees stripped of bark
EF5	Above 200 mph (322 km/h)	Total destruction: catastrophic, widespread damage

EXTREME TORNADO STORY

On the afternoon of 22 May 2011, the city of Joplin, Missouri, was hit by one of the worst tornado disasters in American history. Warning sirens went off 24 minutes before the tornado struck, but many people took no notice – after all, there had been many false alarms. But this one was for real.

UNBELIEVABLE!
The strike on Joplin was so sudden and so devastating that people were left in total shock. One rescue worker was approached by a dazed-looking man, who asked. "When are they going to turn my power back on?" But his house had been completely destroyed.

FLATTENED
The damage was done by winds that ripped through the town at speeds of 400 km/h (250 mph), meaning that the tornado was likely to have been an EF5 category. In the flattened hospital, the remains of a large truck were found — it had been carried 115 m (375 ft) and wrapped round a tree stripped of its bark!

BEFORE AND AFTER
Before the tornado hit, Joplin was a quiet town of 50,000 people, with many solid brick buildings that had stood for over a century. But minutes later, up to 7,000 buildings had been reduced entirely to rubble. It was as if an atomic bomb had fallen.

STORM TRACK

The tornado sliced a mile-wide path of devastation through Joplin. Zack Rosenburg, who helped with rebuilding, said, "The track of that tornado was crystal clear. One side of the street would be completely devastated and the other side of the street had no damage at all."

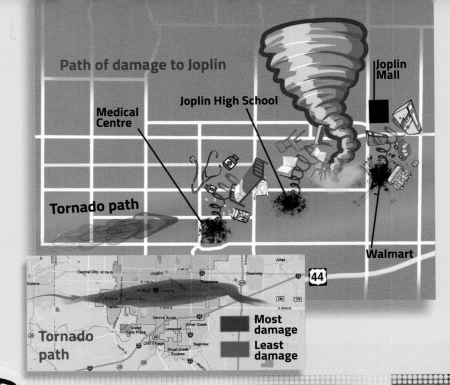

Path of damage to Joplin

Joplin Mall

Joplin High School

Medical Centre

Tornado path

Walmart

Tornado path

Most damage

Least damage

EXTREMES

The Joplin tornado was the seventh deadliest in US history, killing 161 people. The damage done in just a few minutes was so devastating that most experts accorded it an EF5 rating. Trucks and concrete blocks were hurled hundreds of metres, indicating wind speeds of over 320 km/h (200 mph).

PRESS ON!

REBUILDING

Don Attebury, aged 89 years, was one of many Joplin residents whose home was destroyed (above). But afterwards the city embarked on a remarkable rebuilding programme, and by 2016 it was hard to see that the tornado had ever happened. Don Attebury's house itself looked as good as new.

ONE STEP AHEAD OF THE TORNADO

In the last half-century, our understanding of tornadoes has increased dramatically, thanks in part to brave storm chasers. Some storm chasers are photographers hoping to capture amazing shots. Others, such as the scientists of the VORTEX2 and ROTATE2012 projects, are hunting for data that will indicate what conditions trigger tornadoes.

EYEWITNESS

"If I close my eyes I can still hear the sound. It was something I'll never forget – like a high-pitched whistling noise and a low rumble at the same time." Storm chaser Steve Johnson, on coming very close to a tornado...

CAN BIRDS HEAR TORNADOES COMING?

In 2014, scientists noticed that five little golden-winged warblers they were tracking suddenly fled from their nest sites. A day later, a tornado struck. After a few days, with the tornado past, the birds returned safely to their nests. Scientists believe their ultra-sensitive hearing picked up the sound of the tornado in the distance.

TORNADO WARNING

In the 1950s, sirens were set up in many places to warn of air raids in times of danger. Now they are used to warn people a tornado is on its way. Mind you, they don't give you much warning: 13 minutes on average. But that could be just enough for you to get to a place of safety!

THE SOUND OF A TORNADO

Doppler radars have become crucial in tracking tornados. Like conventional radar, they detect things by sending out radio waves and seeing how they bounce back. But Doppler radar can detect which way a storm is moving, as well as its position, from changes in the frequency of waves bounced off water droplets in the storm cloud.

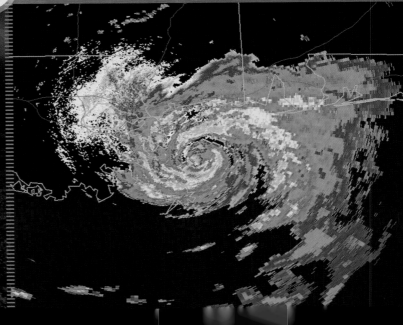

TORNADO CHASERS

American filmmaker Sean Casey became famous for his exploits in the TV series Storm Chaser. To get close enough to the action, he built two armour-plated 'Tornado Intercept Vehicles' (TIVs), with a camera turret, weather sensors, bulletproof windows, and drop-down metal skirts to protect the underside of the vehicle against tornado missiles.

INTENSE FUTURES

This century has seen a number of extreme storms, from Hurricane Katrina to Cyclone Nargis, which killed 138,000 people in Myanmar in 2008. But many scientists believe we are in for even more severe storms. Climate change – the changes in the world's climate triggered by polluting gases such as carbon dioxide – may give the atmosphere extra energy and disrupt weather patterns.

RISING COSTS

Eight of the 10 costliest hurricanes on record in the USA have occurred since 2004. Hurricanes Katrina (2005) cost $108 billion and Sandy (2012) $65 billion, while Hurricanes Andrew (1992) and Ike (2008) cost $25 billion each. That's partly because more people are now living near the sea, but storms also seem to be becoming more ferocious.

TORNADO CLUSTERS

Over the last decade or so, scientists have noticed a change in the pattern of tornadoes. While the number has stayed much the same, tornadoes now seem to be coming in devastating clusters, with long gaps in between. Just such a cluster brought the Joplin tornado of 2011. Some scientists think climate change may be to blame.

STORMY WEATHER

Hurricanes are getting more frequent. Between 1966 and 2009, there were on average six full-blown hurricanes each year. Since 2009, there have been eight hurricanes a year. This is because the ocean has become much warmer. Scientists are not sure why the ocean is warmer, but many believe it is due to climate change.

DANGEROUS BABY

'El Niño' is the Spanish for 'baby boy'. It is also the name of a powerful climate event triggered by changes in ocean currents in the Southern Pacific. Every seven years or so, warm water piles up in the east of the ocean against South America. The result is more extreme weather around the world. Some scientists think climate change may make El Niño effects even more extreme, bringing more intense storms.

TIMELINE

1054
The earliest recorded tornado in Europe struck Rosdalla, near Kilbeggan, Ireland

1609
A hurricane wrecked the settlers' ship *Sea Venture* (left) on Bermuda, inspiring Shakespeare's famous play *The Tempest*

1281
The Hakata Bay Typhoon in Japan wiped out the entire Mongol fleet, earning it the name Kamikaze or 'divine wind'

1780
The Great Hurricane, one of the deadliest Atlantic hurricanes ever, killed nearly 30,000 people in the Caribbean

1635
The Great Colonial Hurricane was the first known New England Hurricane

1815
The Great September Gale hit New England

1054 •

1559
A hurricane destroyed the first colony in Florida

1839
The Coringa Cyclone hit south-east India with devastating effect, killing nearly 300,000 people

1494
Columbus made the first European record of a hurricane. He first sailed to the Americas in the *Santa Maria* (replica shown)

1737
The Hooghly River Cyclone, which hit Bengal, was one of the deadliest storms ever, killing over 350,000 people and destroying 20,000 ships

1881
The Haiphong Typhoon in the Gulf of Tonkin, in the South China Sea, killed 300,000 with its storm surge

1667
The worst ever hurricane in Virginia destroyed 10,000 houses

1974

A Super Outbreak of tornadoes in the USA unleashed 148 tornadoes in just 24 hours

2011

President Barack Obama meets the people of Joplin, devastated by a deadly tornado

1925

The Tri-State Tornado, which hit Missouri, Illinois and Indiana, was one of the biggest and most ferocious ever

1992

Hurricane Andrew was the third most expensive hurricane in US history, causing $25 billion damage in Dade County, Florida

1923

Tokyo was destroyed in the fire whipped up by a typhoon that followed an earthquake

1988

Hurricane Gilbert was one of the most intense storms ever, causing terrible damage in Central America

2005

Hurricane Katrina was the most expensive hurricane ever, devastating the city of New Orleans

2011

1970

The Great Bhola Cyclone killed 500,000 people in Bangladesh, making it the worst natural disaster ever

1989

The world's deadliest tornado hit Daulatpur-Saturia in Bangladesh, killing 1,300 people

1975

Super Typhoon Nina burst major dams in China, driving 11 million people from their homes with the flood

1900

The Galveston Hurricane in Texas was the worst ever to hit America, swamping the city with its storm surge

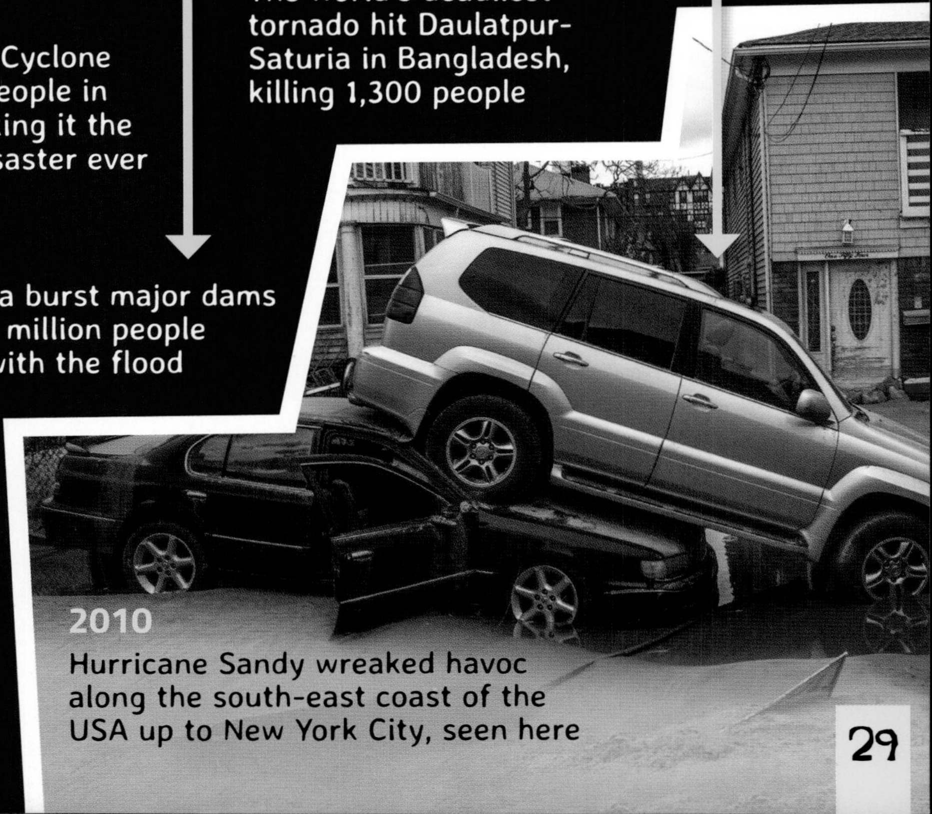

2010

Hurricane Sandy wreaked havoc along the south-east coast of the USA up to New York City, seen here

BLOWN AWAY!

Amazing facts about hurricanes and tornadoes

PICK-UPS

There is a story that in Oklahoma, a small herd of cattle were sucked up by a tornado then set down unharmed some distance away. It probably isn't true. But in April 2011, a boy was said to have been plucked from his bed and dumped a few hundred yards from home. Such escapes are rare.

THE DADDY OF THEM ALL

The largest and most powerful hurricanes on Earth may be 1,600 km (1,000 miles) across, and have winds of 320 km/h (200 mph). That's pretty awesome. But on Jupiter there is a storm twice as wide as the entire Earth, with winds of more than 640 km/h (400 mph). What's more, it's been going on at least 150 years. It's called the Great Red Spot.

NAME YOUR STORM!

Every hurricane, cyclone and typhoon is given its own name to help forecasters as they track it. Hurricanes were first given names by an Australian weather forecaster named Clement Wragge in the early 1900s. The first hurricane of the year is given a name beginning with the letter A. When a hurricane is especially devastating, its name is permanently retired and another name replaces it.

BUSTED!

Some people will tell you that you should open windows to let a tornado through safely. This is a myth. Opening the wrong windows can allow air to rush in and blow the house apart from the inside.

PROJECT STORMFURY

Between 1962 and 1983, the US government flew planes over hurricanes in Project Stormfury. The idea was to drop silver iodide dust into the clouds to act as seeds for raindrops to grow and cool the hurricane. The idea didn't work.

EVIL SPIRITS

Tornado comes from the Spanish word *tornada*, meaning thunderstorm. The word hurricane comes from a Taino Native American word, *hurucane*. It means the evil spirit of the wind.

WORST CYCLONES

WORLD'S DEADLIEST
The Great Bhola Cyclone (Bangladesh)
12 November 1970
Cost in lives: up to 500,000

MOST EXPENSIVE HURRICANE
Hurricane Katrina (USA)
29-31 August 2005
Cost in lives: 1,836
Financial cost: $108 billion

STRONGEST WINDS
Cyclone Olivia (Australia)
10 April 1996
Wind speed: 408 km/h (253 mph)

WETTEST
Cyclone Hyacinthe (Indian Ocean)
14-28 January 1980
Rainfall: 6,083 mm (239.5 in)

DEADLIEST HURRICANE
Great Hurricane of 1780
(Caribbean islands, Puerto Rico)
9-20 October 1780
Cost in lives: 27,000 or more

WORST TORNADOES

WORLD'S DEADLIEST
Daulatpur-Saturia (Bangladesh)
28 April 1989
Cost in lives: 1,300

AMERICA'S DEADLIEST
Tristate Twister (Missouri, Illinois, Indiana)
18 March 1925
Cost in lives: 695

MOST EXPENSIVE
2011 Super Outbreak
(Alabama, Mississippi and other states)
25-28 April 2011
Cost in lives: 348
Financial cost: $11 billion

BIGGEST RECORDED
El Reno (Oklahoma)
31 May 2013
Distance across: 4.2 km (2.6 miles)

STRONGEST WINDS
Bridge Creek-Moore (Oklahoma)
3 May 1999
Wind speed: 484 km/h (301 mph)

INDEX

THE AUTHOR

John Farndon is Royal Literary Fellow at City&Guilds in London, UK, and the author of a huge number of books for adults and children on science, technology and nature, including such international best-sellers as *Do Not Open* and *Do You Think You're Clever?* He has been shortlisted six times for the Royal Society's Young People's Book Prize for a science book, with titles such as *How the Earth Works, What Happens When?* and *Project Body* (2016).

Picture Credits (abbreviations: t = top; b = bottom; c = centre; l = left; r = right)
© www.shutterstock.com:
1 c, 3 tl, 7 c, 9 t, 12 c, 15 cr, 16 b, 20 c, 21 tr, 21 bl, 25 tr, 26-27 c, 30 c, 31 r.
28 tr = © Solodov Aleksey / Shutterstock, Inc, 28 bl = © Holger Wulschlaeger / Shutterstock, Inc, 29 br © MISHELLA / Shutterstock, Inc

Wiki Commons:
13 bl Courtesy the NOAA Photo Library, 25 br © Hello32020

Nasa:
15 tr, 17 tl

2, cl = Deco / Alamy Stock Photo. 4, c = Ronnie Chua / Alamy Stock Photo. 6, c = Stocktrek Images, Inc. / Alamy Stock Photo. 8, c = REUTERS / Alamy Stock Photo. 10, c = Xinhua / Alamy Stock Photo. 11, cl = Xinhua / Alamy Stock Photo. 13, cl = Carol Lee / Alamy Stock Photo. 13, tr = epa european pressphoto agency b.v. / Alamy Stock Photo. 14/15, b = REUTERS / Alamy Stock Photo. 15, tr = NASA. 17, cl = NASA. 17, tr = RGB Ventures / SuperStock / Alamy Stock Photo. 18, c = Deco / Alamy Stock Photo. 22, c = ZUMA Press Inc / Alamy Stock Photo. 22, br = jay goebel / Alamy Stock Photo. 23, cl = epa european pressphoto agency b.v. / Alamy Stock Photo.23, br = Ryan McGinnis / Alamy Stock Photo. 24, c = Ryan McGinnis / Alamy Stock Photo. 25. Cl = Nature Photographers Ltd / Alamy Stock Photo. 27, br = William Brooks / Alamy Stock Photo. 29, tr = REUTERS / Alamy Stock Photo. 31, tr = Stocktrek Images, Inc. / Alamy Stock Photo